W9-APS-181

DISCARDED

VICKI COBB
and KATHY DARLING

WANNA BET?

SCIENCE CHALLENGES TO FOOL YOU

Illustrated by Meredith Johnson

Lothrop, Lee & Shepard Books   New York

THIS BOOK IS DEDICATED TO HELEN KELLER,
who beat all the odds

Printed in the United States of America

First Edition   2   3   4   5   6   7   8   9   10

Library of Congress Cataloging in Publication
Cobb, Vicki. Wanna bet? : science challenges bound to fool you / by Vicki Cobb and Kathy Darling ; illustrated by Meredith Johnson. p. cm. Summary: Provides instructions for a variety of scientific tricks or challenges, such as slicing an apple in midair with a hammer or tying a knot in a chicken bone. ISBN 0-688-11213-7 1. Scientific recreations—Juvenile literature. [1. Scientific recreations. 2. Magic tricks.] I. Darling, Kathy. II. Johnson, Meredith, ill. III. Title. IV. Title: Wanna bet?   Q164.C53 1992   793.8—dc20   92-8962 CIP AC

CONTENTS

A WINNING STREAK

Wanna bet you *can't* do any trick in this book without trying another? These tricks look like long shots, but they're not. We've set them up so that no matter how impossible they seem, you always come out on top. That's the best part of these tricks. There's no question about it, winning is fun.

Creating this book was fun, too. Kathy went over to Vicki's house to play. We played with TV clickers. We blew bubbles, sent each other secret messages, stabbed balloons, made nutty putty, tied bones in knots, ripped apart disposable diapers, munched Life Savers, and set nuts on fire. We laughed a lot. No doubt other grown-ups would think we were weird. Too bad for them. We know fun when we're having it. We figure you do, too.

What you might not know is that the winning formulas in this book are all fixed by scientific principles. The natural world was once a huge mystery that people tried to explain with myths and stories. Then people started studying nature by using careful observation and experimentation, methods that have come to be known as science. Little by little, scientists uncovered secrets of the natural world. Along the way there were surprises and unexpected discoveries that still fool people who are not in the know. There are also some fantastic *un*natural foolers in our high-tech modern world.

The payoff for knowing nature's ways and using scientific information is that you are a guaranteed winner. You could even become addicted to science. In fact, there's such a good chance that we feel compelled to issue the following warning: Caution! These tricks can be habit forming.

Let the power of knowledge go to your head. Turn your friends into believers. Astonish your parents. Teach your teacher a lesson. You'll always have the upper hand, but everyone will have a good time. We'll bet on that.

1
FOOLING YOURSELF

You are not as well connected as you think you are. Your body is made up of a lot of parts and communication among them is sometimes less than perfect. Funny things can happen on the way to the brain. You can be tricked into seeing spots that aren't really there, and in our version of a truly tasteless joke, an apple seems to be a potato.

There are some "brainless" tricks as well. Some messages aren't sent through the brain. That doesn't mean that they can't get screwed up. Muscles can act as if they have a mind of their own, making moves that are out of your control. And in a real brain bypass, the spinal cord can be tricked to give you a fake fright.

On the other hand, you're better connected in some ways than you thought you were. Would you believe your upper lip has a direct link to your temperature sensors? So does your heart. Brainless connections also exist between your nose and your ears.

There are so many ways you can be fooled, you shouldn't trust yourself. But, trust us. Our collection of mixed-up messages will connect with your funny bone. Wanna bet?

WIDE-EYED

Wanna bet you can make your pupils bigger by squeezing your neck!

The setup: This trick requires a subject, a watcher, and a pincher. So that the pupils are small, have the subject face a bright light. The watcher should look into the subject's eyes as the pincher lightly squeezes the back of the subject's neck. If you pinch the right spot, the pupils open wide. The right spot is the place on your neck where your hair stands up when you're frightened. For most people, it's the center of the neck where the hairline ends.

The fix: This is a fake fright. Your body is reacting the same way it does when you need to fight or to run away. You feel a rush as a chemical called *adrenaline* stimulates your nervous system. One reaction to adrenaline is that your pupils get bigger to let in more light, so you can see better. The nerve that controls this is close to the skin at the back of your neck. Pinching this area fires the nerve, producing the same effect in your pupils as adrenaline.

The effect is more dramatic when the pupils start out as small as possible. That's why you begin by looking into a light.

Stand in front of a mirror and try this on yourself. It could be a frightening experience.

COLDHEARTED

Wanna bet ice makes your heart beat faster!

The setup: For this trick you need a bowl of ice water and a watch with a second hand. Take your own pulse by putting two fingers on the inside of your wrist just below the thumb. You should be able to feel your heart beating in the artery that passes close to the surface of your skin. Count the number of beats that occur in fifteen seconds. Multiply that number by four to determine your heart rate per minute. This is your pulse.

Place your hand in the bowl of ice water for one minute—no longer! Take your hand out of the water and immediately take your pulse again.

The fix: The ice-water treatment should raise your pulse about ten beats per minute. Here's why. Ice water causes the blood vessels in your hand to become smaller, and it's harder for the blood to get through. In response, your heart pumps faster. It reacts as if your entire body were cold. But you can trick your heart only for about a minute. After that, your heart catches on and resumes its original rate.

BEE STRONG

Wanna bet a fistful of honey makes your arm more powerful!

The setup: This is a honey of a two-person trick. Put about two tablespoons of sugar in a large square of plastic wrap. Twist the wrap securely around the sugar. Do the same thing with two tablespoons of honey.

Make a fist around the bag of sugar and extend your arm to the side, at shoulder height. Have your partner face you and place one palm on top of your outstretched arm, near your elbow, with his or her other hand resting on the shoulder of your sugar-free arm. Squeeze the sugar and try to keep your arm horizontal while your partner tries to push it down. Repeat the big squeeze with the honey packet.

The fix: It is much easier to push down the arm loaded with sugar. Sugar grains can be compressed, or packed closer together. So some of the squeezer's force is diverted into compressing the sugar. Honey, like most liquids, is not compressible. More strength is available to keep your arm up. Sweetness has nothing to do with success.

BLOOD-SUCKING EARS

Wanna bet you can use your ears to get rid of a red nose!

The setup: To do this, you need a red nose, the kind cold weather gives you in winter. To get the red out, just rub your ears briskly with your hands.

The fix: Your nose becomes colder than the rest of your face because it sticks out. Blood rushes in to warm it up, making it red. Rubbing makes blood rush to your ears. They steal the nearest extra blood, which, when you're cold, happens to be in your nose. Someone should have told Rudolph.

OFF THE WALL?

Wanna bet you can't stand up!

The setup: Stand with your toes against a wall. Then step back four foot-lengths. With your feet together, lean as far as you can toward the wall, catching yourself with your hands. Rest your forehead against the wall and place your hands at your sides. Now try to stand up. If you don't move your hands or your feet, you will never be upright again.

The fix: This trick pits your muscle power against the force of gravity. The places where you are supported are called your *bases*. (When you are standing, your feet are your base.) Instead of pulling on all of your body parts equally, gravity acts as if all the matter of your body is focused in one spot called your *center of gravity*. When you are standing, your center of gravity is directly over your feet. That's why you don't topple.

When you are leaning against the wall, your center of gravity is between two bases, your head and your feet. In order to stand up straight, you must bring your center of gravity over your feet. When you can't use your hands and feet, only your back muscles are available to pull you erect. They're simply not strong enough. Sorry, but we're going to have to leave you up against it this time.

TOTALLY TASTELESS

Wanna bet you can't taste the difference between an apple, an onion, and a potato!

The setup: Put on a blindfold and hold your nose. Have a friend put a small piece of apple, potato, or onion on the center of your tongue. Try to identify it just by taste. No chewing allowed. Now do the same thing with small pieces of the other two things. You will discover a mystery in your mouth.

The fix: Learning how tasteless you are may be hard to swallow. Your tongue is able to identify only four tastes: salt, sweet, sour, and bitter. The identifying organs, called *taste buds,* are not spread evenly over the tongue. The center, where you placed the test materials, has fewer taste buds than other parts of the tongue.

What we think of as taste is really a combination of taste, smell, and texture or "mouth feel" of foods. This trick eliminates the smell and feel clues, and it leaves only the bitter taste of defeat.

Another taste tricker to try: Eat an apple while you hold a cut pear under your nose.

LIP SERVICE

Wanna bet you can use your upper lip as a temperature detector!

The setup: You need three coins in a plastic container and a friend. While your back is turned, have your friend take a coin out of the container, hold it for thirty seconds, and return it. You cannot tell which coin was handled by looking at them. But the answer is right under your nose. Hold each coin in turn against the skin above your upper lip. Your built-in heat sensors will detect the handled coin every time.

The fix: There are many nerves in the skin under your nose that are sensitive to temperature. This part of your body is even more sensitive than your fingers. A plastic container is essential to this trick because it is an insulator. The heat of the coin doesn't escape as quickly in a plastic container as it would in a metal one.

A HANDOUT

Wanna bet only one hand will move from the center of a yardstick when you try to part your hands!

The setup: In *Bet You Can't* we challenged you to try to make your fingers meet under a yardstick at any place but the center. It couldn't be done. We've recently discovered there's more to this trick than we originally thought. The second part is even more mysterious.

Balance a ruler 12 to 36 inches long with the center resting on both of your outstretched index fingers. Slowly move your fingers apart. Surprisingly, only one hand moves.

The fix: In the original trick the meeting place of your hands was determined by the stick's center of gravity. The same forces are operating when you move your hands apart. Your body has a complicated feedback system, called *proprioception,* that automatically coordinates your body movements and keeps the stick in balance. Notice, only one hand moves at a time. This happens because the moving hand requires something to pull against in order to move. The friction between the stationary hand and the ruler is the force the moving hand pulls against.

When you move your hands apart quickly, things change. Speed reduces friction. Now both hands can be moving at the same time. However, the hand with the least amount of friction moves farther.

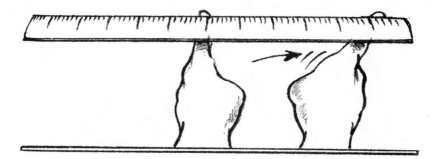

FALSE MOVES

Wanna bet you can move cardboard just by staring at it!

The setup: You can't really move paper by staring at it, but this illusion is so powerful that it really seems to move. In this case, seeing is not believing. Fold an unlined 3" × 5" index card in half lengthwise. Place the folded card on a table so that one end of the card faces you and the fold is at the top, like a pup tent. Your eyes should be slightly above the level of the card. Close one eye and stare at a spot in the center of the fold. Stare hard. For a while, you will see the card as you positioned it. Then, suddenly, the card will appear to be standing on end. Keep on staring the same way at the standing card illusion. Move your head slowly from side to side. The card will appear to sway back and forth.

The fix: The illusion of the dancing cardboard tricks you in two ways. Closing one eye removes some of your ability to judge depth, so the folded cardboard doesn't appear to be three dimensional. The brain doesn't have enough information to judge whether the fold is bent toward you or away from you. The brain switches back and forth between the two possibilities. When the card appears to be standing up, the depth cues are reversed: the fold, which is really closer to you, now seems to be the farthest point from your eye. Now the motion illusion can occur.

Normally, when you move your head, you change your point of view, and the foreground appears to move faster than the background. As you move your head in front of the reversed-form illusion, the edges (which appear to be closer) seem to be moving faster than the fold (which appears farther away) and the whole illusion seems to sway.

GRAY GHOSTS

Wanna bet you can see gray where there is no gray?

The setup: Stare at one of the black boxes in figure 1. Ghostly gray spots will appear at the intersections of the white lines. To be a ghostbuster, stare at one of the white intersections. That gray ghost will disappear, although ghosts will continue to haunt the other intersections.

Now stare at one of the white boxes in figure 2. They're haunted, too. Very faint gray spots will appear in the black intersections.

Figure 1

The fix: These are brightness illusions. White appears whiter when it is next to black, and black appears blacker when it is next to white. At the intersections of the white lines, white appears to be meeting white, producing the illusion of something less than white—in other words, gray. The same is true when black lines meet black and produce something less than black—gray, again.

When you stare directly at an intersection, the image falls on the center of your eye. The nerve cells there are better at detecting the difference between black and white than are the cells of your peripheral vision. So, no ghost appears.

Figure 2

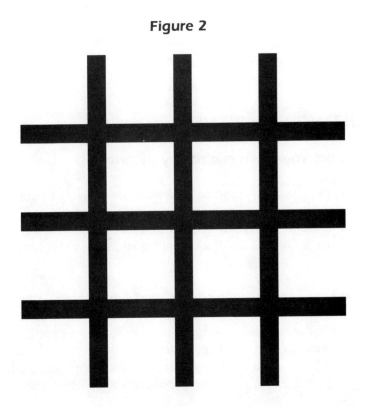

UPLIFTING EXPERIENCE

Wanna bet your arms can rise by themselves!

The setup: Stand in a doorway and place the backs of your hands against the door frame. Press as hard as you can for thirty seconds. Step out of the doorway and relax your arms. Within a few seconds, they will rise automatically. If it doesn't work, do it again longer and harder.

The fix: As you press your hands against the door frame, your nerves tell your muscles to contract and lift your arms. The door frame prevents your arms from moving. When you step away and free your arms, the muscles continue to contract after you have stopped pushing. The only way you'll get this effect is if you keep your brain out of it. If you consciously try to keep your arms from rising, they won't.

26

IT ALL ADDS UP

Wanna bet you can read a message through a slit that only lets you see a slice!

The setup: In a large piece of cardboard, cut a 2-inch-long slit, as narrow as you can possibly make it. Place the cardboard over some writing. Size doesn't matter. Move the slit rapidly back and forth across the page. You'll get the message.

The fix: Your amazing brain puts the pieces together like a jigsaw puzzle. What you are really seeing is a series of slices. When the series appears rapidly enough (fifteen to sixty flashes per second, depending on the brightness of the light), the images fuse, creating a single picture.

NO SWEET TOOTH

Wanna bet an artichoke can make water taste sweet!

The setup: Pour a glass of water. Taste it. Eat a fresh-cooked artichoke (with salt and butter, if you wish). Taste the water again. If you're one of the lucky ones, it will taste sweet.

The fix: Artichokes, which are not sweet, contain a chemical called *cynarin,* which stimulates the same taste buds that sugars stimulate. You need to eat about half an artichoke before these taste buds start firing. They stay fooled even after you've finished eating the artichoke. All food, not only water, tastes sweeter as a result. The effect lasts for a few minutes. Scientific studies have shown that six out of ten of people have this sweet experience. In our experience, Vicki got it but all Kathy got was an overdose of artichoke, not her favorite food.

2
COMMANDING FORCES

I t's game time. Take on the forces of nature. Make the right moves and you win. There are only three simple rules. We're going to give them to you right up front:

1. A resting object will stay put forever and a moving object will keep moving forever unless an outside force acts on them.
2. The way an object moves is determined by the size of the object and the size and direction of the force that hits it.
3. Forces come in pairs. For every action there is an equal and opposite reaction.

How can these straightforward rules possibly make an interesting game? The answer is that the action isn't always easy to follow. The rules have hidden twists. Master them and you'll control the game.

Nature's forces include gravity, friction, and your own muscle power. With our coaching, these forces are yours to command. You can multiply force and be stronger than a weightlifter, absorb force and throw raw eggs across a room without breaking them, divert force and keep a knife from cutting a piece of paper.

We invite you to enter the arena and be a player.

33

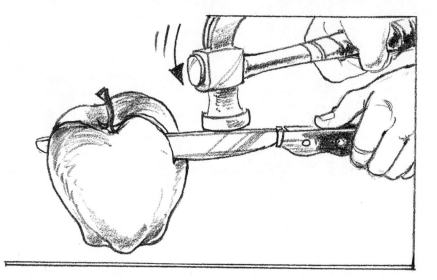

FORCED ENTRY

Wanna bet you can use a hammer to slice an apple in midair!

The setup: Here's one for the apple polishers. Start out as if you were going to slice an apple in half with a table knife. Press the knife in far enough to pick the apple up with it and hold it up at arm's length. With a hammer, give the knife a sharp blow on the back of the blade. Strike as close to the apple as you can. The knife will cut through the rest of the apple, and the two halves will fall to the ground.

The fix: When you cut an apple, you overcome its resistance to being cut. There are two ways to do this: by applying a small force for as long as you need or by applying a large force for a shorter period of time.

When an apple rests on a table it is held steady and all the force goes into the apple. A small force for as long as it takes will get the job done. When the apple is in the air, a larger force is needed or the apple will travel downward with the knife. The blow of the hammer is so large that the resistance to the knife is overcome and the apple splits before it has a chance to travel with the knife.

UNCUTTABLE PAPER

Wanna bet you can slice an apple without cutting the paper wrapped round your knife!

The setup: Fold a piece of paper and place a knife blade in the fold. Cut an apple with the paper-wrapped knife. Use a steady downward pressure rather than a sawing motion. After the apple is split, look at the paper. It will not be damaged.

The fix: A knife can cut both paper and an apple. But it is easier to cut an apple because apple pulp offers less resistance than paper fibers do. The paper-wrapped knife doesn't cut the paper because you're not applying enough force. There's enough to cut the apple but not the paper, and the paper moves with the knife. If you hold the paper against the apple, the unwrapped knife will cut the paper. When you prevent the paper from moving with the knife, you can apply enough force to cut it.

NO HUMPTY DUMPTY HERE!

Wanna bet you can throw a raw egg across the room without breaking it!

The setup: The most difficult part of this trick is to convince a parent to contribute a sheet. It helps if you offer to do the laundry. You won't have to. Trust us.

Have two friends hold up a sheet with enough slack at the bottom to prevent the egg from rolling out after the toss. Choose a raw egg that is free of cracks and throw it as hard as you can at the sheet. Stand at any distance. Throw overhand or underhand, with any speed you want. As long as you don't miss the target, your egg will survive to become an omelet at another time.

The fix: According to Sir Isaac Newton (an "eggspert" in these matters), the force of a collision is determined by the mass of the object and the speed just before it hits. The sheet acts as a brake for your egg missile. It moves with the egg and stops it gradually. The sheet also protects the egg by spreading the force over a large surface area.

Eggs are stronger than you might think. After all, hens sit on them. The shape of the shell resists breaking when a force is evenly applied to the outside. However, a small force applied to the *inside* of the shell cracks it wide open. This design is good for baby chicks!

A LIGHT SNACK

Wanna bet you can make a puffed cheese snack rise through rice!

The setup: Prove that a puffed cheese ball is really a light snack and defy gravity at the same time. All you need is some rice, a glass jar with a lid, and a snack ball. Add rice to the jar until it is about one-quarter full. Place the snack ball on the rice. Put the top on the jar and turn it upside down. Shake the jar from side to side. Do not shake it up and down. The ball will mysteriously rise through the rice.

The fix: When grains of rice are set in motion, they behave more like a liquid than like a solid. An object floats in a liquid when its weight is less than an equal volume of the liquid. A snack ball weighs a lot less than an equal volume of rice. When you shake the rice, the motion gives it a buoyant force and the snack ball "floats" to the surface.

If you don't have cheese snacks handy, try popcorn, a styrofoam ball, a cork, or a Ping-Pong ball.

Buoyancy isn't always an upper. Wanna bet you can shake down an object, such as a marble, that's heavier than an equal volume of rice?

FINANCIAL SUPPORT

Wanna bet you can support eight quarters on a dollar bill suspended between two glasses!

The setup: If you think it's better to have folding money than coins, this trick's for you. The U.S. dollar has hidden strength that even bankers might find surprising. Fold a crisp, new dollar bill in half lengthwise. Then fold both lengthwise edges up to meet the center crease. The dollar will be folded like an accordion. Make a bridge between two glasses with the dollar bill. Arrange eight quarters along the length of your dollar bridge.

The fix: The "corrugated" dollar is amazingly strong. Ordinarily, a dollar bill supported only at its ends will not support the weight of even *one* quarter. The weight of the coin is greater than the structural strength of the dollar bridge. Pleating the bill redistributes the weight of the coins so that it is spread out. Now, the bill is able to support the coins. It's a secret strength that has lots of everyday applications.

Diverting the lines of force gives added strength to many materials. An I-shaped steel beam is as strong as a much thicker solid rod. This allows skyscrapers to be built with a lot less weight. Cartons are constructed with a corrugated sheet of cardboard sandwiched between two flat sheets of cardboard to make them sturdy. Wanna bet you can support yourself with a lot less money than you thought possible!

FAST FORWARD

Wanna bet a balloon can go faster than a car!

The setup: Tie a helium-filled balloon inside a car so that it doesn't touch the roof. When the driver speeds up, you feel as if you're being pressed backward into your seat. The balloon, however, moves forward. The speed-demon balloon is stopped only by the string or the windshield of the car—or maybe by an annoyed driver.

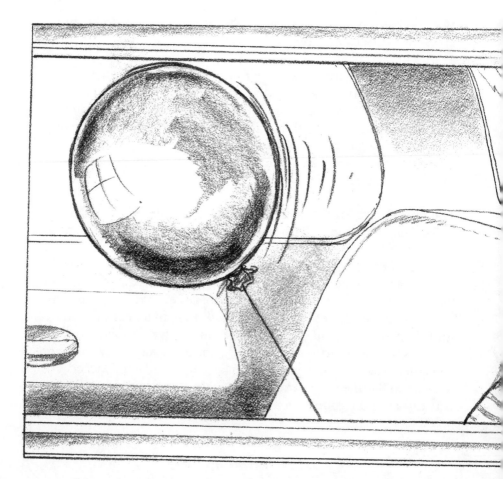

The fix: The balloon moves opposite to everything else in the car. If the car turns left, you're pushed to the right, and loose balls roll to the right, but the balloon leans to the left. Here's what's happening. When the car speeds up, you are not actually moving backward; it only appears that way to you. You can think of the seat moving forward so that it presses against your back. In the same way, the air in the car pushes the balloon forward from the rear. Since the balloon is lighter than air, the force of the air gives it a shove forward. Since there is very little resistance (the balloon is not in contact with any part of the car), the balloon keeps moving at a speed slightly faster than the car's.

LIGHTEN UP!

Wanna bet you can lose weight in one second!

The setup: This is the quickest trick in the book. You can lose a lot of weight with our split-second weight-loss program. Here's how. Stand on a bathroom scale and note your weight. Quickly bend your knees while you watch the scale. As your body moves down, the pounds disappear. When we tried this, one of us, who will be nameless, lost 150 pounds—and then rocketed up to 250 pounds, which is as far as the scale registered. Fortunately, neither condition lasted too long.

The fix: When you bend your knees quickly, for a split second the weight of your upper body is not supported by your feet. The "weight loss" shows up on the scale. Skiers use this technique and lift their weight off their skis so they can turn.

The moment you end your knee bend, not only do you get back all your original weight, but the sudden stop shows up as additional weight on the scale. The amount gained or lost depends on how fast you bend your knees. The faster you bend them, the more you lighten up—and fatten up!

RAW POWER

Wanna bet you can't stop a spinning egg!

The setup: This trick requires raw power, so make sure you use an uncooked egg. Place it on its side on a tabletop and spin it vigorously. Stop the spinning egg but let go of it immediately. It will begin spinning again all by itself.

The fix: This is not a case of an egg with a memory! The spin on this trick is the liquid inside the egg. When you stopped the shell from moving, you didn't stop the liquid. As soon as you released the shell, the moving liquid set the whole egg in motion again.

A hard-boiled egg with its solid contents acts as if it is all shell. When you stop it, it stays stopped.

BIONIC ARM

Wanna bet you can't lift my hand from the top of my head!

The setup: Sit down and place your open hand on top of your head. Spread your fingers as wide apart as possible and hang on to your head. Here we go! Have a friend grip your forearm as close to your elbow as possible and try to lift your hand off your head. Use a straight upward pull with no sudden movements. Your "bionic" arm can't be moved.

The fix: Surprise, your arm is a machine! It's a simple machine, but nevertheless a machine (which is any device that increases your strength or your speed). In this case your arm is a lever. Here's how it works. The force required to lift your hand is greatest next to your elbow and least next to your wrist. To lift your hand from this position, the lifter would have to be three or four times stronger than you are. Your mechanical advantage is considerably less when the lift is at your wrist.

NO STRINGS

Wanna bet a yo-yo will climb a string no one is holding!

The setup: This is the world's greatest yo-yo trick. No kidding. You can make a yo-yo defy gravity and climb up the string after you let go. It takes a little practice to master, but it's worth it.

Make a yo-yo "sleep." (If you don't know how, consult a local yo-yo pro.) Then take the string off your finger and hold it between your thumb and forefinger. Now slap your hand while you watch the yo-yo. As soon as it starts to come up the string, let go. The yo-yo will charge up the string. Catch it in your hand. Some professionals use this trick to end their act, catching the wound-up yo-yo in their pocket.

The fix: When a yo-yo sleeps there is almost no friction between the string and the spinning axle of the yo-yo. A jerk on the string increases the contact between the string and the axle, creating enough friction to rewind the string. A slap is a stronger, quicker force than you normally give with wrist action, and the rewind is quick enough to be completed before the string has a chance to fall.

3
MATTER OF MYSTERY

Five hundred years ago, Columbus discovered the natives of a Caribbean island playing with balls made out of something quite mysterious. Unlike balls the Europeans had seen before, these balls bounced! The natives made the bouncing balls from the sap of a tree. They also dipped their feet in the sap. When it dried, their feet were waterproof. This bouncy, waterproof stuff is probably not a mystery to you. It's good old rubber.

It took a different kind of explorer, the laboratory scientist, to show how rubber could be put to good use. Natural rubber gets sticky in hot weather and brittle in the cold. Charles Goodyear, in 1839, figured out how to make rubber usable in any temperature.

Scientist-explorers not only alter materials, sometimes they discover brand-new ones. These materials are as mysterious to us as rubber was to Columbus. We've taken some of these high-tech materials and created tricks that exploit their weirdness. Would you believe there's a bouncing liquid, a thirsty powder that drinks eighty times its weight in water, or a metal that can be trained to remember? Investigating the properties of these materials is like entering unknown territory. Explore this chapter and maybe you can discover something in addition to fun.

SPARK-A-PEEL

Wanna bet you can make fireworks with a lemon!

The setup: You need a lighted candle for this trick, so be sure to have an adult nearby before you start. Cut a thin slice of rind off a lemon. Hold the outside of the rind near the flame and squeeze the inside surfaces together. You'll see mini-fireworks between the rind and the candle flame.

The fix: All oils are flammable, and lemon rind contains tiny pockets of oil. When the rind is squeezed, the skin breaks and tiny jets of oil squirt out. Lemon oil burns in a brief but bright sparkle when it is ignited.

OLD NEWS

Wanna bet you can make paper last two hundred years!

The setup: You can write a message to your great-great-great-great-grandchildren or you can preserve today's newspaper for them to read. You'll need our antiaging formula because some paper becomes so brittle that it falls apart when it gets old. The formula for paper preserver is 9 tablespoons of milk of magnesia and 1 quart of club soda. Mix them in a shallow pan and soak your paper in the solution for an hour. Remove it carefully and blot it between sheets of paper towel. Let it air dry. It is possible that this treatment might not last the full two hundred years, but we can't wait to find out.

The fix: In the presence of acid, oxygen breaks down the cellulose fibers of paper. Since acid is used in the manufacture of most paper, it contains the seeds of its own destruction. The antiaging formula contains magnesium carbonate, which forms when the magnesium hydroxide in milk of magnesia combines with the carbon dioxide of club soda. The magnesium carbonate neutralizes whatever acid is present in the paper. It leaves a residue, so any acid that might form in the future will also be neutralized.

BENT OUT OF SHAPE

Wanna bet you can tie a knot in a bone!

The setup: A chicken drumstick bone can be as flexible as a rope—but not without a conditioner. Vinegar is a good one. Place the bone into a jarful and soak it overnight. Test it in the morning. If the bone is still stiff, let it soak some more. When it is good and rubbery, tie your knot.

The fix: Bones are stiff because tiny crystals of calcium compounds are embedded in a framework of flexible protein fibers. Vinegar is an acid. When it combines with the calcium compounds, the mixture forms a new substance that dissolves in the liquid. Only the flexible part of the bone is left. Your ears and nose are made of a similar material called cartilage.

BALLOON ACUPUNCTURE

Wanna bet you can skewer a balloon without popping it!

The setup: Blow up a balloon and let a little air out before you tie it off. There should be a small bulge of unstretched rubber in the "end" opposite the knot. This is your target. Your acupuncture needle is a thin bamboo skewer. Dip the point of the skewer in some oil, for a smooth insertion. Then poke it into the target area, with a gentle twisting motion. The balloon will not pop. Push the skewer clear through the balloon, exiting through the unstretched rubber next to where the neck is tied. Again, no pop.

The fix: As any good acupuncturist knows, it's where you stick the needle that counts. A balloon is made of a thin sheet of rubber. Stretched rubber is weaker and thinner than unstretched. A pinhole in a stretched area of a balloon quickly becomes a tear as air rushes out. The rubber around a hole in an unstretched area is strong enough to resist the force of the escaping air. If you remove the skewer, air will leak slowly out of the tiny holes you have made. Prove that this is no trick balloon. Jab the skewer in the side. Ruptured rubber results! Easier done than said.

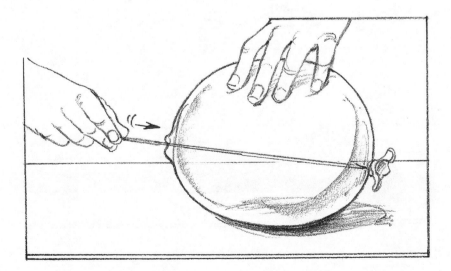

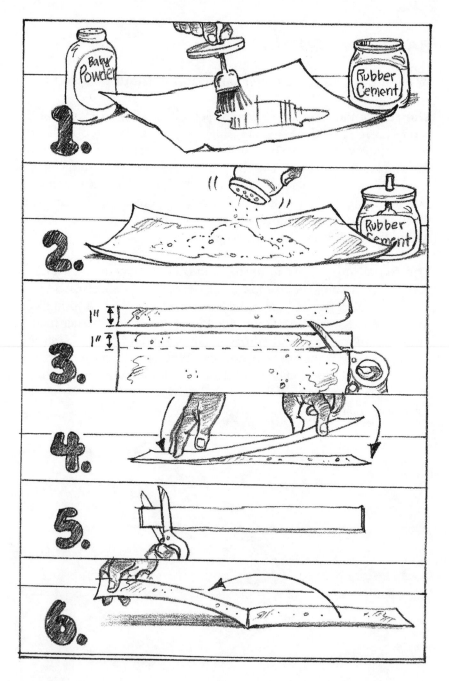

HINGE ON THE FRINGE

Wanna bet you can cut and glue paper at the same time!

The setup: In this trick, as you cut two pieces of paper, the cut edges stick together. First you have to doctor the paper. Spread a thin, even coat of rubber cement on it and allow it to dry. The paper will feel tacky. Spread talcum powder on the paper and gently rub it over all the dried cement.

Cut two one-inch strips from the paper. Place one strip over the other with the powdered sides touching. With a sharp pair of scissors, cut across the strips close to the end. Press the cut ends together, or just wait for a minute, to make sure the cement sticks. Then, holding the uncut end of the top strip, gently raise it. Instead of two strips, you'll find that you have one long one. If you cut the two strips on a 45-degree diagonal, they will form a right angle when you raise the top strip.

The fix: The talcum powder covers the cement so that the strips do not stick together. When you cut the strips, you expose glue at the freshly cut edge. Molecules of rubber cement have a strong attraction for one another. They form a hinge strong enough to hold the strips together.

POWER OF MONEY

Wanna bet you can attract a dollar with a magnet!

The setup: Hold a dollar bill by one end. Bring a strong magnet near the other end. The bill will be attracted to the magnet.

The fix: The ink used for United States currency is made with chemicals that contain iron. As everyone knows, magnets attract iron. Dollar-changing machines have a magnetic sensor that "reads" the pattern of the ink on bills. It rejects forgeries, as well as old bills from which some of the ink has been worn off.

MUNCHABLE METAL

Wanna bet there are iron filings in your breakfast cereal!

The setup: Iron is good enough to eat. In fact, you do eat it. Breakfast cereal manufacturers often add bits of iron to their products. The pure iron is ground up so fine that you don't notice it in the cereal, but a magnet can remove it.

Empty a packet of iron-enriched instant Cream of Wheat into a plastic bag. Place a clean magnet in the bag. Shake well for a few minutes. As you remove the magnet, try to touch as little of the magnetic surface as possible. If you look closely, you'll see tiny iron filings clinging to the magnet. Carefully wipe the particles onto a sheet of white paper. To see them well, put the magnet under the paper and move it around to make the filings "dance." You will collect only a tiny amount, which is your body's total daily requirement.

The fix: Who would have thought you could eat pure iron, the stuff people pump in the gym? *Hemoglobin,* the red protein in the blood that carries oxygen, must have iron to do its job. Since the pure metal can be used as easily as iron compounds, the government permits very fine iron filings to be added to food. The words "iron fortified" on the package simply mean that ground-up iron has been added to the cereal.

We've heard that you can remove iron embedded in some flaked cereals, such as Total. Crush the flakes and add water. Then go fishing with your magnet.

NUTTY PUTTY

**Wanna bet you can transform glue into something
completely useless but fun!**

The setup: In the early 1940s, a substance was invented that was so
weird it couldn't be classified. In some ways it's like a liquid. In others
it's like a solid. It flows. It bounces. It stretches when pulled slowly
but breaks when pulled quickly. Its inventor called it "Nutty Putty,"
and you can make your own version.

Recipe for Nutty Putty

1 tablespoon borax (you can get borax in the detergent section
  of a supermarket)
1 tablespoon white glue (such as Elmer's)
1 cup plus 1 tablespoon water

Put the glue in a small container. Mix in one tablespoon of water.
In another container, dissolve the borax in a cup of water. Add a
tablespoon of the borax solution to the diluted glue and stir. Nutty
Putty happens.

The fix: Nutty Putty was created by General Electric scientists who were trying to make an inexpensive substitute for rubber. Nutty Putty, a flexible goo, stretched farther, bounced higher, and resisted mold and decay better than rubber. However, there were a few drawbacks. It never held a shape and it broke when you hit it.

It did make a small fortune as a toy called Silly Putty. Lots of people wrote letters to the manufacturer with suggestions on how to use it. It could lift print off newspaper, collect cat fur and lint, clean ink off typewriter keys, and level wobbly furniture. But after more than fifty years, no one, including some of the world's leading engineers, ever came up with a really practical use for it.

Our version is not exactly the same as commercial Silly Putty, but it has the same properties. White glue is made up of long, stringlike molecules called *polymers*. These molecules are so long that they interfere with each other, making the glue thick and slow to pour. Borax cross-links the polymer chains together. Cross-linked polymers get even more tangled, trap water, and form a gellike material. The substance has new properties that make it fun to play with.

ELEPHANT WIRE

Wanna bet a wire remembers its shape!

The setup: Elephants never forget and neither do some wires. A wire with a built-in memory is used by orthodontists for braces. Ask your orthodontist or dentist for a piece of nitinol arch wire so that you can see metal memory in action.

Arch wire is programmed to remember the U shape of your jaw. Bend it and twist it into a different shape. Pour some hot tap water into a container. Drop the twisted arch wire into the hot water. With the speed of sound (720 miles per hour), it will pop back into its original shape.

The fix: Nitinol is a high-tech material made of two ordinary metals: nickel and titanium. The process by which they are combined gives nitinol three unique properties: It "remembers" its original shape and will quickly spring back when heat is applied; it stretches one hundred times more than ordinary wire; it absorbs sound.

It is great for braces because it stretches and then remembers its original shape. Braces made of nitinol never have to be tightened

when the teeth move. Arch wire has only a one-way memory, but memory metals can be "trained" to have a two-way memory. Springs made from them are placed in shower heads. When the water gets hot enough to scald you, the spring opens and cuts off the water. When the water cools, the spring "remembers" its closed position and lets the water flow again. Its sound-absorbing property is used to make machinery less noisy. Maybe you can suggest school bells be made from nitinol. They will never ring!

Your arch wire is an "untrained" wire. To get a two-way memory you have to train it. Here's how. Get a nut and a bolt. Wrap the wire around the bolt and make a spring. Tighten the nut so that it clamps the wire. Dip it in a bowl of hot water and then in a bowl of cold water. Repeat the water treatment fifty or more times. The amount of training your metal will need depends on the difference between the temperatures of the two bowls of water, but fifty double dips should do it. Take the nut and the wire spring off the bolt. Now when you dip the wire in the hot water it will take the original shape of the arch, and when you dip it into the cold water it will form the coiled spring.

Plastics with a memory have just been developed. They have many of the unusual properties of memory metals. We were going to include a trick with them, but we forgot.

SUPER-SLURPER

Wanna bet you can't pour water out of a glass!

The setup: The secret of this trick is a superslurping plastic you can get out of a disposable diaper. To collect the super absorbent, cut the edges off a toddler-sized disposable diaper. Discard the plastic covering. Rip the padding into small pieces and put them into a large plastic bag. Seal the bag and shake it. After a few minutes, remove the padding. There will be about one-half teaspoon of grainy powder in the bottom of the bag. The best way to get it out of the bag is to shake it into a corner and cut off the corner.

Place the powder in a small glass. Add about one third cup of water. Wait a few minutes. Turn the glass over. Ta da! Nothing pours out.

The fix: The superabsorbent plastic in the diaper is called sodium polyacrylate. It can absorb about eighty times its own weight in liquid by trapping water molecules in a gel. Diaper ads on television show water being poured into the diapers. Since salt makes polyacrylate less absorbent and urine is salty, the ads are a bit deceptive. Add salt to your gel and check this out yourself.

Superslurpers are also used to help hold water in the soil around the roots of plants.

4

FLUID FAKEOUTS

Go with the flow! The earth is covered by two fluids, air and water, and they are constantly flowing. A fluid is a gas or liquid that moves and changes shape—a con artist's dream. They do unexpected things. Air is especially tricky because its moves are invisible.

Most people are so familiar with air and water that they don't expect surprises. An egg climbing up a waterfall sure surprised us—a case of going *against* the flow. Most people think a bubble will break when you poke it. We've got a fluid fooler guaranteed *not* to burst your bubble.

Of course, nothing surprises Mother Nature. There are natural laws that account for all the behavior of fluids, strange or otherwise. It's the loopholes in those laws that will let you fake your friends out.

Con games depend on inside information. This chapter is overflowing with it.

TAP-DANCING EGG

Wanna bet you can make an egg climb a waterfall!

The setup: Use the nearest waterfall. Make it in your kitchen sink. Fill a glass with water and put a raw egg in it. Notice that the egg sinks. (If it doesn't, it's rotten.) Place the glass under your kitchen waterfall. The stream doesn't push the egg against the bottom of the glass as you might expect. Instead, the egg not only rises to the top of the glass but actually travels up the stream above the rim of the glass.

The fix: This is a real fooler. Scientists have not been able to explain exactly why it works. We do know that the water must be very turbulent. Without violently rushing water, the egg will only rise to the top of the glass. Turbulence causes it to climb the waterfall. You may have to experiment a bit with the flow to get the effect eggsactly right.

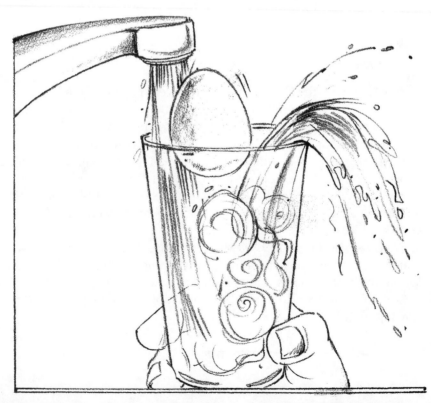

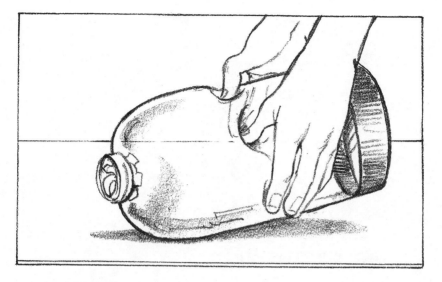

SUCKER BET

Wanna bet a bottle will suck up a wad of paper!

The setup: In *Bet You Can't!* we challenged you to blow a piece of paper into an empty soda bottle. We told you to rest an empty soda bottle on its side, place a small wad of paper in the neck, and try to blow the paper into the bottle. We were right—it didn't work.

You can't do it with your breath, but the forces of Nature can. The catch is in the setup, which is just a little bit different. You must use a plastic bottle. Squeeze the bottle in the middle to make a dent. Hold the bottle horizontally and place the wad of paper in the neck. Squeeze the soda bottle to make the dent pop out. The wad of paper flies into the bottle. Don't blink, because the bottle is one fast sucker.

The fix: Denting the bottle gives it a smaller volume. A dented bottle contains less air than an undented one, and some of the air is forced out. There's a well-known saying that Nature hates a vacuum. When you release the dent, you create a partial vacuum. When the bottle returns to its original shape and volume, there is less air in it. Instantly, air from the room rushes into the bottle to fill the partial vacuum. It carries the lightweight paper wad with it.

MESSAGES IN THE MIST

Wanna bet you can write with a potato!

The setup: Future spies, take note. You can write secret messages with a piece of raw potato. Cut a potato and write on your bathroom mirror with the cut surface. The message will be practically invisible until someone takes a shower. Then the message appears in the misty mirror.

The fix: This is nothing to get steamed up about. Water vapor forms tiny droplets when it comes in contact with a cool mirror. Droplets form because the force of attraction between the water molecules is stronger than the attraction between the water molecules and the glass molecules. This clouds the mirror and you can't see in it.

The raw potato contains a substance that the water molecules "like" almost as much as they "like" each other. Instead of forming little balls that reflect light, the water vapor over the message forms a thin sheet that's easy to see through. The writing appears as clear areas surrounded by the foggy dew.

It is possible to use potatoes as emergency windshield wipers. If your wipers break, rub a piece of raw potato across the windshield and the raindrops will turn into thin sheets of water that you can see through.

DON'T TAKE THIS LYING DOWN

Wanna bet you can make a cork float upright!

The setup: Try to place a cork in a bowl of water so it floats on its end. Don't waste a lot of time. The cork will float only on its side. But this rule applies only to a single cork. You can get a cork to float upright if it's part of a group. Here's how. Hold three or more corks underwater until they are thoroughly wet. Gather them in an upright position at the surface of the water. Make sure the sides are touching each other. Slowly remove your fingers. The cork raft will float with all the members upright.

The fix: A single cork floats on its side because its center of gravity is at its lowest point in this position. If you gather the corks together, they float upright because, for a raft, this is the position where the center of gravity is lowest. In this trick, water acts like glue. The water is attracted to the surface of the corks and also to itself. The bond that forms is strong enough to create the raft.

POKING FUN

Wanna bet you can stick your finger through a soap bubble without popping it!

The setup: Soap bubbles are about the thinnest thing you can see with the unaided eye. Because they are thin, they are fragile. You can't stick your hand though one without bursting your bubble. Not unless you make a "bubble" with a hole in it. We know a way to do it.

You will need some bubble solution and a "magic" wand. Any bubble solution will do. Buy it or make it with our recipe. The wand, however, is special. Bend some wire into a large circle. Make a circle of thread a little larger than your finger. Suspend it in the center of the wand by attaching it with strings at opposite points on the wire circle. Pour bubble solution into a shallow pan and dip the wand into it. Remove the wand, making sure there's a film of soap on it, and pierce the film in the loop of thread with a pencil. The loop of thread springs open, forming a circular hole you can stick your finger through.

Recipe for bubble liquid

⅓ cup dishwashing liquid (Joy or Ajax works well)
a few drops of glycerine (optional)
1 quart warm water

Mix the dishwashing liquid in the water. Adding the glycerine will produce longer-lasting and stronger bubbles.

The fix: The thread loop forms a barrier that prevents the entire soap-film "bubble" from bursting. The thread opens into a circle because the soap film pulls evenly all around it.

LITE DETECTOR

Wanna bet you can pick a can of regular cola from a can of diet cola blindfolded!

The setup: This is a science experiment you can drink after you are finished. You will need a can of regular cola and a diet cola of the same brand. Make sure the cans are identical. Fill the bathtub to a depth of at least eight inches. Put on a blindfold and get a friend to hand you the two cans. Hold both cans underwater with the bottoms resting on the tub. Let go. The can of diet cola will float higher than the regular cola. You can feel the difference, even with your eyes covered.

The fix: Believe it or not, diet drinks really are lighter! When you read the label you will see that each can contains the same number of fluid ounces. Fluid ounces are a measure of volume, not weight, though. A twelve-ounce can of regular cola contains about ten teaspoons of sugar. They dissolve in the liquid without increasing its volume. The molecules of sugar spread evenly between the water molecules, where there's a lot of empty space. There are now more molecules in the cola, making the liquid more dense. Diet colas are usually sweetened with aspartame, which is 160 times sweeter than sugar. Obviously, ten teaspoons of sugar weigh more than a pinch of aspartame. The cans are the same size but the densities are different. The can that contains the lower-density liquid will float higher.

There is one other way you can tell the two colas apart. Ask a bee. Bees are not the least bit interested in the diet cola. They must not worry about their weight.

EGG BEATER

Wanna bet you can make an egg stand on end!

The setup: Try to stand a raw egg on end. Can't do it, can you? It *is* possible, but you have to scramble the egg inside its shell. Shake it vigorously for several minutes. Then hold it for a few seconds with the bigger end on a table. Carefully remove your hand. Ta da! The egg is standing on its end. If it isn't, shake some more and try again.

The fix: An egg normally rests on its side. In this position the center of gravity is closest to the shell.

Weight is not evenly distributed inside an egg. The yolk is denser than the white, and there's a tiny pocket of air at the broad end. But the center of gravity is pretty close to the geometric center of the egg because the yolk is held in place by two twisted strands of protein that anchor it to the shell. When you shake the egg, one of two things happens: either the yolk breaks free and sinks or all the contents, including the air, become scrambled. In either case, the contents are now free to flow inside the egg. When you hold the egg upright, the center of gravity shifts, and you can then balance it on its end. It takes a few seconds for the contents to settle and the air to rise to the top.

THICK AND THIN

Wanna bet you can take the stiffness out of library paste!

The setup: Library paste is weird stuff. Open a jar. It looks solid, impossible to stir. Try anyhow. The harder you stir, the easier it gets. Soon the stiffness disappears.

The fix: Quicksand and library paste have a lot in common. They both become more fluid the more you stir them. This strange property is called *thixotropy*. When a force is applied to a thixotropic fluid, it flows more easily. When you stop the force, it returns to its original consistency. Thixotropic properties are useful in library paste because when you apply force to spread it, it flows more easily. This same property in quicksand, on the other hand, puts your life in danger. The more you struggle, the more liquid the ground becomes. Beware of quicksand but be glad for thixotropy in ketchup, mayonnaise, honey, and dripless paints.

SHOWING YOUR TRUE COLORS

Wanna bet iodine is violet, not brown!

The setup: Check with an adult before you do this trick because iodine is poisonous. If you ever put iodine on a cut, the first thing you felt was its sting. Then you probably noticed (as you were blowing on your wound) that it left a brown stain. It might surprise you to know that iodine is not really brown but violet. In fact, *iodine* comes from the Greek word for the color violet.

To make iodine show its true color, you'll need some greasy kid stuff—baby oil. You will also need a clear glass jar with a screw top. Half-fill the jar with water. Add iodine until the solution is the color of tea. Pour an inch of baby oil on the surface of the water. Screw the lid on and shake. When the liquids separate, the oil will have a beautiful, violet color. Iodine is now showing its true color!

The fix: Pure iodine won't dissolve in either alcohol or water. To make the alcohol solution called tincture of iodine, which is what you find in your medicine chest, chemists have a trick. They use an iodine compound, sodium iodide, that does dissolve in water and alcohol. It can carry pure iodine along with it. A water-alcohol mixture of sodium iodide and iodine is brown. But pure iodine *is* soluble in oil, as the bright violet color proves.

Fluids don't all have the same properties. Scientists take advantage of the differences when separating materials that are mixtures. In this case, the pure iodine was extracted from the water solution with the oil. Since oil floats to the surface, it can be separated from the water.

5

ENERGY SHOCKERS

Big shocker! There will never be more energy on earth than there is right now. But you don't need to alert the media—the planet is *not* going to run out of it. In fact, there won't ever be any less than there is right now. So why, then, is everybody going around crying that there is a crisis and telling us to save energy?

Even though energy can't be created or destroyed, it can be changed from one form to another. Heat, light, sound, electricity, the energy in molecules (called *chemical energy*), and that in atoms (called *nuclear energy*) are all forms of energy. When people talk about the energy crisis, what they're really talking about is running out of fossil fuels. These are the natural gas, oil, and coal that formed millions of years ago from decaying plants and animals. Engineers and scientists know how to transform fossil fuels into energy we can use. They haven't yet figured out enough inexpensive, renewable, nonpolluting alternatives to fossil fuels to meet future energy requirements.

We're working on transforming energy ourselves. So far, we've managed to convert some heat, light, and sound into entertainment. We're going to teach you how to make electric spit. That ought to warm you up so you can create lightning in your mouth. Then we'll introduce you to a renewable fuel source that's pretty nutty.

These tricks may not contain an answer to the world's energy needs, but they will generate watts of fun.

VAMPIRE FIRE

Wanna bet you can make fire with blood!

The setup: Dracula didn't invent this trick, but he would have loved it! Since it requires the use of fire, have a grown-up stand by.

Pour about an inch of hydrogen peroxide into a wide-mouthed glass container. Light a long wooden skewer or match, blow out the flame, and hold the glowing end close to the surface of the peroxide. Nothing happens, right? Peroxide alone won't affect a glowing stick. You need to make a bloody mess before it will burst into flame.

Now for the gory part. You need a source of blood! Add a pinch of very fresh (bright red) hamburger or a piece of fresh liver to the peroxide. Light the stick again and blow it out. Put the ember near the now bubbling peroxide and it will burst into flame.

The fix: Fire is energy that results when a fuel (in this case, wood) combines with heat and oxygen. Air is only about 20% oxygen. If you increase the amount of oxygen, the energy is released faster.

Hydrogen peroxide contains a lot of oxygen that is very unstable. If you look closely, you can see tiny bubbles of oxygen as they slowly move to the surface. Blood (yours included) contains an enzyme, called *catalase,* that speeds up the release of the oxygen, turning the peroxide into plain water. Oxygen bubbles out of the peroxide so rapidly that it forms a froth as it escapes into the air. In the oxygen-rich environment, the dying fire blazes again.

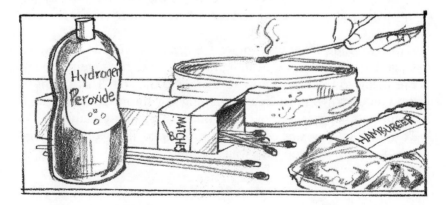

SWEETNESS AND LIGHT

Wanna bet sugar glows in the dark!

The setup: This should spark your interest. You can make mini-lightning with cubes of sugar. Take two sugar cubes into a closet or a very dark room. It is very important to wait five to ten minutes so your eyes can adapt to the darkness. Rub the two cubes rapidly together or strike one against the other as if you were striking a match. You will see a faint glow where the cubes meet.

The fix: The glow is lightning on a very small scale. Lightning is a stream of electricity that excites nitrogen molecules in the air. Excited nitrogen releases as light the extra energy it gets from the electricity. When sugar crystals are crushed, the pieces become positively and negatively charged. That makes the electricity jump through the air between the pieces of sugar, exciting nitrogen molecules and making them emit light.

Chemical energy is stored in all kinds of molecules. In some substances, chemical energy can be changed to light energy by pressure. Sugar crystals have this unusual property. When you squeeze, press, or crush the crystals, they give off electricity called *piezoelectricity* (*piezo* means pressure).

More energy is released from the sugar than meets the eye. The next trick taps into this invisible energy and is guaranteed not to leave you in the dark.

THE ELECTRIC LIFESAVER

Wanna bet you can make sparks fly in your mouth!

The setup: Rubbing sugar cubes may not be one of the all-time great tricks, but candy that flashes lightning in your mouth is. You've gotta try this one—you may develop quite a taste for it.

Again, you must go into a dark room and wait for your eyes to adapt to the darkness. You can observe the mouth lightning with a mirror or take turns creating it with a friend. Hold a Wint O Green Life Saver between your teeth and watch as you bite it. Sparks of blue-green light leap out wherever your teeth crack the candy. If you are not allowed to bite hard candies, use a pair of pliers.

The fix: This trick begins where the last one left off. The same scientific principle is working here. Piezoelectric sugar in the candy provides the energy. Some of it is emitted as the glow you saw in the sugar-cube experiment, but a lot of it is released as ultraviolet light that the human eye can't detect. Wintergreen is a substance that absorbs the ultraviolet energy and transforms it into visible light. This process is called *fluorescence.* The excited wintergreen molecules emit a bright blue-green light that is stronger than the glow from sugar alone.

The same phenomenon is at work in certain adhesives. Rip apart a Curad bandage wrapper in the dark. Green light flashes from the strips as the glue is torn apart. The adhesive contains the necessary sugar and fluorescent material.

This trick will not work with candies made with sugar substitutes. You'll get no light from lite candy!

A NUT CASE

Wanna bet you can toast a marshmallow with a nut!

The setup: When you consider the high price of oil, you might not think it grows on trees. Surprise, it does! This is a nutty trick, but we are not crazy when we suggest burning a Brazil nut. Nuts contain oil, and a single, shelled Brazil nut burns long enough to toast several marshmallows.

Since this trick involves fire, have an adult present. Stick a Brazil nut on the triangular, pointed end of a metal can opener and place it in the center of a pan. Light a long candle or a fireplace match and hold it under the nut until it begins to burn, then extinguish the candle or match. Wait until the nut is burning steadily before you toast your marshmallow.

The fix: Brazil nuts are large seeds that are 67 percent oil. Brazil-nut trees use the energy of sunlight to manufacture oil. The oil is a source of stored chemical energy that can be released later. The Brazil-nut seedling uses this energy to grow. When you eat a Brazil nut, your body uses this energy. You can also release the energy stored in oil by burning it. The light energy of the sun can be transformed into energy used by living things or into the heat and light of fire.

Brazil nuts are not the only oily nuts. You might want to try toasting marshmallows with a walnut, a cashew, or even a macadamia nut.

Unlike petroleum, nut oils are a renewable resource. Theoretically, there could be peanut-powered cars in our future.

ELECTRONIC SPIT

Wanna bet you can taste electricity!

The setup: Although this trick involves electricity, it is not a shocker. Believe it or not, electricity has a flavor all its own. To find out what it tastes like, you will need aluminum foil and a piece of silver. Touch the foil to the tip of your tongue. Then taste the silver. Notice the flavor of each. Put them together and touch your tongue to the place where they overlap. The tangy taste that tingles your tongue is electricity.

The fix: You have made a battery with your tongue. Batteries produce electricity, a stream of tiny negatively charged particles called *electrons.* In your tongue battery, electrons move from the aluminum through your saliva to the silver and then directly back to the aluminum. As the moving electrons cross your tongue, they stimulate the nerves in your taste buds. Now that you have tasted power, are you hungry for more?

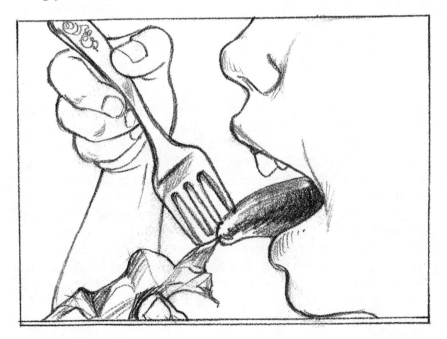

A SICK JOKE

Wanna bet you can fake a fever with a TV clicker or a flashlight!

The setup: Thermometer strips are an inexpensive, modern way to take your temperature. You can get them in almost any pharmacy. When you place one against your forehead, it changes color, showing whether or not you have a fever.

You can make these strips register a fever even when you don't have one. Try placing a TV remote-control device against the thermometer strip and clicking the on-off switch. Vicki's clicker didn't work, but Kathy's did. So, if yours doesn't work, shine a small flashlight on the strip instead, and you may get the same hot news.

The fix: Sometimes it takes high tech to beat high tech. The temperature strip contains an unusual kind of matter, a liquid crystal.

Normally a crystal is a solid. Ice, diamonds, emeralds, and salt are examples of crystals. The molecules in all crystals have a regular arrangement that scatters the light that strikes them. Sometimes scattered light gives a crystal its color. When a crystal melts and changes into a liquid, the molecules are no longer held rigidly in a regular pattern and the crystal no longer scatters light the same way.

A liquid crystal has a regular arrangement of molecules like a solid, but it also flows like a liquid. When heat energy is applied to the liquid crystal, the structure of the molecules continually changes. Each change scatters a different color of light. So you see the chemical go through a series of colors: red, yellow, green, blue, and violet. When it cools, the colors show up in reverse order. Heat, however, is not the only kind of energy that will affect the liquid crystal. Infrared radiation that comes from the TV clicker and ordinary light from a flashlight also do the job.

NOTHING TO GET STEAMED UP ABOUT

Wanna bet you can't boil water in boiling water!

The setup: There's an old saying that a watched pot never boils. That's because it seems to take forever to come to a boil when you're in a hurry. But in this trick it *would* take forever. The water truly never boils.

Have an adult present while you do this trick, since you will be using the stove. Put some water into a glass jar. Find a way to suspend the jar in a pot of water so that it doesn't touch the sides or the bottom. If you use a two-handled pot, hang the jar from a wire that is fastened to the handles. Heat the pot on the stove. The water in the pot will soon come to a boil, but the water in the jar never will.

The fix: This may come as a bit of a surprise. After all, the water in the jar is the same as the water in the pot. To make water boil and turn into steam requires an input of heat energy. The heat energy of the stove makes the temperature of the water in the pot rise until it reaches 100 degrees Celsius (212° F). At that point, the stove's heat changes the water into steam—the water boils. The conversion of water to steam keeps the temperature from rising above 100° C. The water in the jar, however, is kept separated from the source heat, the stove. So it never gets enough heat to boil.

A double boiler works on this principle. It is used to cook foods that should not boil, like chocolate pudding.

6

LIGHT
ENTERTAINMENT

Step right up and meet Light—one of the most amazing performers of all time. Thrill as it moves faster than anything else in the universe. Marvel at its acrobatic bends and bounces. Watch it rotate through a rainbow.

For your entertainment, Light will flip your favorite TV show upside down and allow you to read inside a sealed envelope. Meet Invisible Light: Infrared and Ultraviolet. Ultraviolet will reveal secret messages written with laundry detergent and sunscreen lotion. Infrared takes command of your TV set.

The Light Show includes guest appearances by Mirrors and Lenses, who play featured roles. As magical as our Light Entertainments seem, they are based on the science of optics. We won't keep you in the dark any longer. We want you to see the light!

A TV FLOP

Wanna bet you can watch TV upside down on a piece of paper!

The setup: You can turn any TV show into a flop. All you need is a magnifying glass and a piece of white paper. Turn the tube on and cut the lights. Stand about ten feet from the set and hold the magnifying glass between the television and the paper. Both the paper and the magnifying lens should face the screen and be vertical. Position the paper about six inches from the lens. Now move the lens back and forth until you see a focused image of your TV picture projected on the paper.

The fix: Your image is tiny, upside down, and backward. The magnifying glass bends light that passes through it and focuses the emerging light to form an image. The light from the left side of the screen is bent to the right, light from the top of the TV is bent to the bottom, and vice versa.

100

HOME-GROWN TV

Wanna bet you can make a big-screen TV with a shaving mirror!

The setup: Can't afford a big-screen TV? Why not grow it yourself? Here's how you can get the big picture. All you need is an ordinary television with a wall behind it and a magnifying shaving or makeup mirror at least six inches across. Turn the TV on and the lights off. Hold the shaving mirror about two feet in front of the screen and tilt it slightly upward to project the image on the wall. To focus the image, move the mirror either closer or farther away from the TV. Moving the TV away from the wall will let you make an even bigger picture.

The fix: There's one very good reason why this home-grown large-screen TV hasn't caught on. You'll notice it immediately. This is yet another flop. Your favorite program is upside down and backward.

A magnifying mirror has a curved surface. Like all mirrors, it reflects light. But the curved surface spreads the reflected light so that it projects an enlarged image. Any mirror reverses left and right, but the curved mirror also reverses top and bottom.

FAR-OUT REMOTE CONTROL

Wanna bet you can control your TV from another room!

The setup: For this trick you need a television with a remote-control unit, several mirrors, and some friends. Notice that the front panel of the TV has a small square or circular light detector. This is your target. Stand outside the TV room. Have a friend hold a mirror so that you can see the TV in the mirror. Aim the remote control at the image in the mirror. Fire! The TV obeys your command.

The fix: The remote control device is an invisible-ray gun that shoots infrared light. This invisible light bounces, or reflects, off a mirror, just like the light you can see. The reflection of light from a mirror is very predictable. If *you* can see a person in a mirror, that person can also see you in the mirror. The light detector in the TV is like an eye. If you can see the TV in the mirror, it will get the message sent by the infrared beam. You can make your remote control even more remote. Just add mirrors and friends to hold them. If everything is properly lined up, there's no telling how far you can go.

NO PLACE TO HIDE

Wanna bet you can see through a mirror!

The setup: For this trick you will need a pair of mirrored sunglasses. Normally when you look at someone wearing mirrored sunglasses, you see the whites of your own eyes, not theirs. It is possible to see through these mirrors, though. Just put a light behind them. What were once impenetrable mirrors are now transparent.

The fix: Most mirrors don't transmit light. They only reflect the light that strikes their surfaces. Mirrored sunglasses, however, have a special surface that allows light to pass through. (If they didn't, they wouldn't be much use as glasses.)

They are not one-way mirrors. There's no such thing. If light can go through one way, it can go through the other way, too. When people wear mirrored sunglasses, there is isn't enough light between their eyes and the lenses for you to see their eyes from the mirrored side. If you hold the mirrored side to your eyes, though, you'll see right through. The transparency of either side depends on where the greatest amount of light is.

Two-way mirrors have been used to con people for years. When magicians make objects appear and disappear, it's often done with the aid of these mirrors. They also make an ideal "cover" for spies. To check out suspicious mirrors, turn out the lights and put your eye right up to the mirror.

READING OTHER PEOPLE'S MAIL

Wanna bet you can read a letter through the envelope!

The setup: It's the business of spies to see things other people don't want them to see. A good spy knows how to read a message without opening the envelope. It is illegal to read other people's mail. Spies don't care. We'll show you how to do it, but we don't want you to get into trouble—and blame us. Have a friend write you a message and seal it in an envelope. You can read the message right through the envelope if you spray it with hair spray or artist's fixative spray (matte-finish Krylon).

The fix: Light passes through transparent materials. Although it is made of two transparent materials, cellulose fibers and air, paper is not transparent. That's because light travels at different speeds through different transparent materials. When it passes from one transparent material to another, it bends at the boundary because of the different speeds. (That's why the magnifying glass focuses the image of your TV screen.) Instead of passing through paper, light is bent at the boundaries of cellulose and air and scatters internally. When you spray the envelope with a fixative, the air spaces are filled with a material that transmits light at about the same speed as cellulose. The light has a more uniform material to pass through, so it doesn't bend and scatter. The paper becomes transparent.

Oil makes paper transparent for the same reason, but a spy wouldn't use oil because the envelope would remain transparent. Tampering would be obvious. Hair spray evaporates quickly and doesn't leave a clue.

THE MILKY WAY

Wanna bet you can see a sunset in a glass of water!

The setup: Ever wonder why the sky is blue and sunsets are red? Create your own milky way to discover the answers. Stir ½ teaspoon of milk into an 8-ounce glass of water. Shine a flashlight through the side of the glass. Notice the bluish color of the water-milk mixture. Now look directly at the flashlight bulb through the side of the glass. It looks yellow. Shine the flashlight up through the bottom of the glass. When you look down on the flashlight bulb from the surface of the liquid, it looks orange.

The fix: The milk-water mixture is a model of the atmosphere. The earth's atmosphere is made up of gas molecules, water vapor, and dust particles. When light travels through the atmosphere, the particles scatter the light. Sunlight is white light that is made up of all the colors of the rainbow, called the *spectrum.* Blue light is scattered the most, making the sky appear blue. The milk particles, suspended in the water, scatter blue light from the flashlight in the same manner.

When you see the sun during the day, you see what's left of the spectrum after the sky has scattered the blue light; the remaining light from the sun's surface is actually a mix of green, yellow, orange, and red, but it appears yellow.

The sun is closest to you at noon, when it's directly overhead. At sunset the sun is near the horizon. Now the light source is farther from you, and sunlight has to pass through more of the atmosphere and it hits more particles. Not only the blue but the green and yellow light are scattered as well, leaving behind an orange or red sun. When you look at the flashlight from the top of the glass, the light passes through more of the mixture than it does from the side. More colors are scattered, leaving behind an orange bulb—a sunset in your glass.

COLOR BLIND

Wanna bet you can't find a blue gum ball!

The setup: Put gum balls of different colors (white, red, blue, green, etc.) in a box. View them through a filter made of eight layers of red cellophane. The red gum ball and all the other colors that reflect a lot of light will appear white. The green and blue gum balls will look black.

The fix: When white light strikes a red object, the object reflects the red part of the spectrum and absorbs all the other colors. When you look through a red filter, the light you see is red; all the other colors have been filtered out. When the red light strikes the red gum ball, most of the light is reflected and you see it as white. When red light strikes a blue gum ball, there is almost no blue light for the gum ball to reflect. All the red light is absorbed and it appears black. Green gum balls also look black. You won't be able to tell the blue from the green. There's no need, however, for others to know of your defeat. Eat the evidence!

TIME OUT

Wanna bet you can make time disappear!

The setup: To do this trick you need a pair of polarized sunglasses and a watch with a liquid crystal display (LCD). Put the sunglasses on and look at the time display. Slowly rotate the watch and the numbers will magically disappear. Keep turning and they'll reappear again.

The fix: Light travels in all directions. Polarized sunglasses are filters that pass only light that's traveling in a vertical direction. Most glare is polarized light that travels horizontally. It is stopped by the vertical polarized lenses, which are at a right angle to it. The top of a liquid crystal display has a polarizer on it. You can't see the numbers on the watch when your polarized glasses are aligned at right angles to the watch's polarizer.

Substitute an LCD calculator for the watch and instead of killing time you can eliminate math.

AH, SWEET MYSTERY OF LIGHT

Wanna bet there's a rainbow hidden in syrup!

The setup: All the colors of the rainbow can be seen in a glass of clear corn syrup. To see the light show, you need two polarized lenses from sunglasses (check with the owner before you pop the lenses), a clear glass, Karo syrup, a light source, and a helper.

Look down at the light source through one lens, the drinking glass, and the second lens. Rotate the top lens until you find the darkest position. Keep looking while your helper slowly pours syrup into the glass. One by one, beginning with blue, the colors of the spectrum appear.

The fix: Corn syrup has the ability to rotate polarized light. When you look through two polarized lenses that are rotated so that the directions of polarization are at right angles to each other, all the light is blocked. By adding syrup, light passing through the bottom lens is rotated slightly. This light is no longer at a right angle to the top lens, so some of it passes through. The emerging light shows up as a single color. The color that you see is the one that is rotated into a position that lines up with the top lens. As you increase the thickness of the syrup, you increase the rotation of polarized light so the next color moves into the line-up. When you see red, stop pouring. You're at the end of the spectrum. Now if you rotate the top lens, you will be able to see all the colors again, one by one in order.

There are other optically active syrups. Check out honey and pancake syrups.

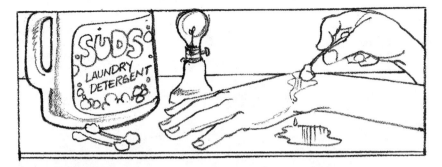

A BRIGHT IDEA

Wanna bet you can write secret messages with laundry detergent!

The setup: You will need colorless liquid laundry detergent that contains brighteners, a "black" light bulb from a hobby or novelty store, and a cotton swab. To write a secret message, use the cotton swab as a pen, the laundry detergent as the ink, and your arm as the paper. When the message dries, it will be invisible. To reveal it, look at your skin under the black light. The message will glow!

The fix: Most laundry detergents contain fluorescent chemicals called brighteners. Although a black light appears dim, it's giving off a lot of light that you can't see, called *ultraviolet*. When ultraviolet light strikes fluorescent materials, it is changed into visible light. That's why the message glows.

Ultraviolet light is present in sunlight. Small particles of the brighteners remain in your clothes after washing. They transform the ultraviolet light from the sun into visible light and make the colors look brighter.

Sunscreen is an ultraviolet blocker. It is designed to protect your skin from the damaging ultraviolet rays of the sun. Instead of fluorescing, like brighteners, it absorbs ultraviolet light. You can use sunscreen lotion to write secret messages, too. White paper is especially striking. Under the black light, the paper, which contains brighteners, glows and the sunscreen message is dark. A message on your skin doesn't show as much contrast, but it can still be read.

7

MATH TRICKERY

If you love math, we've got your number. If math makes you sick, welcome to the club! Math isn't always about counting or adding or multiplying or any of those boring things that your calculator does. The fun in this chapter is *beyond* calculation.

We saved the math chapter for last because we wanted to increase the probability of getting you involved. In fact, the whole theme of this book—winning bets—is a branch of mathematics called probability. We're betting you will probably want to continue your winning streak.

We've used math to create some wildly improbable things, too. A triangle with square corners, paper with only one side, and a loophole in a loophole are not fantasies. They are examples from another branch of mathematics, called topology.

Ever hear of a computer virus? One kind is mathematical. It sets computers going in an endless circle. So be careful when you play with our version; it could infect your PC.

If you get bitten by the math bug, don't count on being cured.

DOUBLE CROSS

Wanna bet you can draw parallel lines that intersect!

The setup: Hold two pens (or pencils) side by side against each other. Place the parallel points on a piece of paper. Move the paper under the pens so that a figure eight is created. Don't tilt the pens; keep them at right angles to the paper at all times. The parallel lines will intersect each other at the center of the figure eight.

The fix: By definition, parallel lines are lines that are always the same distance from each other. This is the one and only requirement of parallel lines.

When most people think of parallel lines, they think of *straight* lines. They are the only parallel lines that can never cross. Curved parallel lines, on the other hand, can double-cross you. The trick to getting a figure eight that has parallel lines is turning the paper as you move it beneath your pens.

A STACKED DECK

Wanna bet shuffling doesn't make a difference when the cards are stacked right!

The setup: Arrange a deck of cards so that the black and red cards alternate. Cut the deck. Make sure the bottom cards are opposite colors. Shuffle the cards once. Deal cards from the top of the deck in pairs. In spite of your shuffle, they will always be red-black pairs.

The fix: You can be a card shark if you use a little mathemagic. What appears to be miraculous is really the result of a math law. It is called the *Gilbreath principle* after the mathematician-magician who formulated it in 1958.

If you don't see the math behind the magic, do the trick with the cards face-side up. Stack your deck and cut it so one red and one black card face up. Imagine you are shuffling the deck. Put one card down to represent the first card to hit the table in your shuffle. If it is black, both halves of the deck will now have a red card up. It doesn't matter which half of the deck supplies the next card. If you put a red on a red, then the next two cards will be black and your red-black pair combination-will be continued.

Figure Eight Möbius Strip

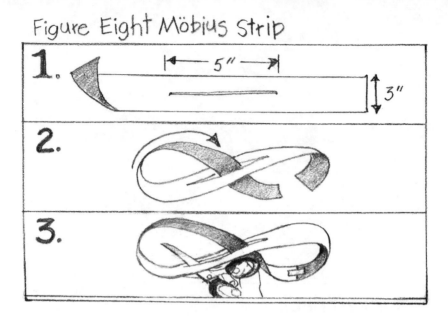

1. |← — 5" — →| ↕ 3"

2.

3.

ONE-SIDED CONTEST

Wanna bet you can cut a figure eight in half so that it forms a single loop!

The setup: You will need some newspaper, scissors, and tape. Cut a long strip of newspaper about three inches wide. Cut a five-inch slit in the center of the strip. Push one end of the paper through the slit and turn the inserted end over to give it a twist. With tape or glue, fasten the top surface of the inserted strip to the bottom surface of the other end of the strip. The completed loop looks like a three-dimensional figure eight.

Cut the figure eight in half by continuing the slit along the center line. As you make the final cut and meet your starting place, the figure eight disappears and you are left holding one big ring of paper.

The fix: In *Bet You Can't!* and *Bet You Can!* we introduced you to the simple yet fabulous weirdness called the *Möbius strip.* A Möbius strip has only one side. See for yourself. Cut another strip of newspaper. Bring the two ends together. Give one end a twist so that you can

Siamese Möbius Strip

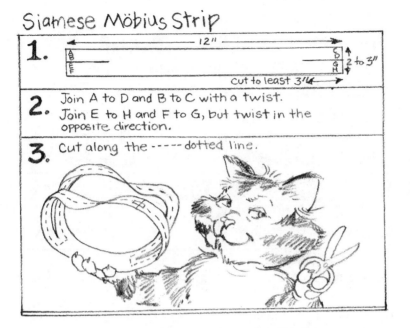

1. ← 12" →
B ─────────────── 6 D
M
E ─────────────── 6 G | 2 to 3"
F
← cut to least 3⁄4 →

2. Join A to D and B to C with a twist.
Join E to H and F to G, but twist in the
opposite direction.

3. Cut along the ----- dotted line.

tape the top surface of one side to the bottom surface of the other.
Draw a pencil line along the center of the strip. You can draw a line
that ends up back where you started without lifting your pencil. This
proves that there is only one continuous surface.

The wonders of a Möbius strip have been immortalized in a poem:

> A mathematician confided
> that a Möbius strip is one-sided.
>   You'll get quite a laugh
>   if you cut it in half,
> for it stays in one piece when divided.

There are many variations of the Möbius strip. The figure-eight
Möbius strip is a little more complicated because the twist passes
through a slit. But cutting it results in the same large loop of a simple
Möbius strip. Topologically speaking, the slit strip is identical to the
simple strip.

Here's another complicated Möbius strip if you're hooked on them.
It's called a Siamese Möbius strip and there are no words to describe
the results. Cut along the dotted lines. But don't get bent out of shape.

119

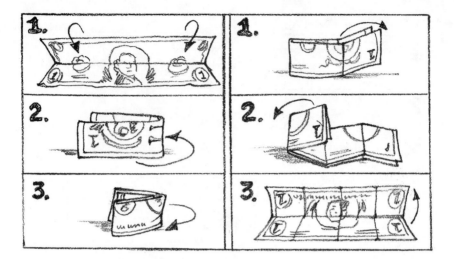

FOLDING MONEY

Wanna bet you can flip George Washington on his head without turning a dollar bill upside down!

The setup: Hold a dollar bill so that the picture of George Washington is facing right side up. To flip him, you must fold the bill in half three times. The sequence of folds is all-important.

Fold 1: the top edge folds forward to meet the bottom edge.

Fold 2: the right edge folds back to meet the left edge.

Fold 3: the right edge folds forward to meet the left edge.

The folding is complete. Now comes the all-important unfolding sequence.

Unfold 1: the back of the left side unfolds toward you.

Unfold 2: the right side opens like a book.

Unfold 3: the bottom edge is lifted up to reveal George standing on his head.

The fix: This trick won't work if you reverse your steps and unfold the bill in the same sequence as you folded it. George flips only if you use a different pattern to unfold. This shows how important proper sequence of operations is in mathematics. In other words, follow orders.

NO END IN SIGHT

Wanna bet you can get trapped in a math game. Start with any number you like, you'll *always* wind up with the number 4!

The setup: Don't try this trick unless you can spell and count. Think of any number in the universe. Write it in numerals. Then write the word and count the letters. Write this number in numerals. Then in words. Keep going. No matter what number you started with, you will end up with four. Every time. Promise.

The fix: Four is the only numeral in the English language in which the number of letters in the word is the same as its numerical value. Count on it.

IT'S ALL RIGHT

Wanna bet you can draw a triangle with three right angles!

The setup: A triangle is a three-sided figure with angles that add up to 180 degrees. A right angle is 90 degrees. Three right angles total 270 degrees. So a triangle with three right angles sounds impossible. And it is, if you draw it on a flat surface. The trick is to draw your "impossible" triangle on a sphere. We suggest marking an inflated balloon with a felt-tip pen.

There are two ways you can make your triangle: (1) Draw the three right angles first. The corners should be set up so that straight lines will connect them to make a triangle with sides about the same length. (2) Draw a right angle and extend one line around about one third of the ball. Make another right angle and extend that line around one third of the ball. Now draw the third right angle and extend the line until you reach your starting point.

The fix: Your triangle enters the third dimension in this trick. The rules of three-dimensional math are not the same as they are for two-dimensional math. Topologists are concerned with the mathematics of form and shape. They are especially interested in the results of stretching and changing surface contours, like what happens to the 3-D triangle when it is reshaped into two dimensions.

Deflate the balloon and you will see that your figure is closer to being a normal triangle. If you could make the rubber perfectly flat, the triangle would have three 60-degree angles and would be a normal triangle.

INDEX

VICKI COBB, a New York City native, received her bachelor's degree in zoology from Barnard College and her master's degree in secondary science education from Columbia University. She has contributed to the field of science education as a high school teacher, researcher, scriptwriter, television show creator and host, and as the author of numerous books. She lives in White Plains, New York.

KATHY DARLING was born in Hudson, New York, and has lived in more than thirty countries. She received her bachelor of science degree in biochemistry from Russell Sage College. She has edited and written many children's books, as well as adult books, and worked as a syndicated columnist and as president and publisher of a specialty publishing company. She lives in Larchmont, New York.

MEREDITH JOHNSON graduated with honors from Art Center College of Design in Los Angeles. She has designed and illustrated a great number of books, and works as an advertising art director as well. Ms. Johnson and her family live in La Cañada, California.